D1570641

Knock-knock.
Who's there?
Hugo.
Hugo who?
Hugo first, I'm scared!

Knock-knock.
Who's there?
Salmon.
Salmon who?
Salmonchanted evening.

Knock-knock.
Who's there?
Wendy.
Wendy who?
Wendy door opens, I'll come in!

500 WACKY KNOCK-KNOCK JOKES

Dora Wood

BALLANTINE BOOKS • NEW YORK

Sale of this book without a front cover may be unauthorized. If this book is coverless, it may have been reported to the publisher as "unsold or destroyed" and neither the author nor the publisher may have received payment for it.

Copyright © 1992 by Dora Wood

All rights reserved under International and Pan-American Copyright Conventions. Published in the United States of America by Ballantine Books, a division of Random House, Inc., New York, and simultaneously in Canada by Random House of Canada Limited, Toronto.

Library of Congress Catalog Card Number: 92-90615

ISBN 0-345-38080-0

Printed in Canada

First Edition: December 1992

Contents

500 WACKY KNOCK-KNOCK JOKES

Introduction

I've always loved knock-knock jokes. They're hilarious. You can tell them to anybody and you can make them up about everybody. You have to be pretty clever to make up good ones, though, and I am always searching for more good knock-knock jokes.

That means I'll try to use anything for a knock-knock joke. I use places I hear about in the news, the names or people I meet or read about in books. I even love to make up jokes with the food I eat. Sometimes I use names or words that are out of the ordinary, because that makes it harder for people to guess the joke. If you don't know that Kyoto is in Japan, you'll still be trying to figure out where it is when I hit you with the punch line.

If you like to tell knock-knock jokes as much as I do, I hope you'll send me a few, because I'm writing some more knock-knock joke collections. If you're the first person to send me your joke, I'll even put your name in the book next to that joke. You can write me at:

Dora Wood
P.O. Box 30373
New York, NY 10011-0104

Some of my friends have already given me some good jokes, and I want to thank them. They are Ron Blaikie, M.F. Green, Michael Moore, and Charlie P. Sartwell. Thanks a lot, guys!

2

Shirley, You're Joking— Girls' Names

Knock-knock.
Who's there?
Agnes.
Agnes who?
Agnes and Topeka and the Santa Fe!

Knock-knock.
Who's there?
Alison.
Alison who?
Alison it's dark outside!

Knock-knock.
Who's there?
Alma.
Alma who?
Almany knock-knock jokes can you take?

Knock-knock.
Who's there?
Augusta.
Augusta who?
Augusta go home now!

Knock-knock.
Who's there?
Enid.
Enid who?
Enid some more allowance!

Knock-knock.
Who's there?
Willa.
Willa who?
Willa you marry me?

Knock-knock.
Who's there?
Jewel.
Jewel who?
Jewel know me when you see me!

Knock-knock.
Who's there?
Harriet.
Harriet who?
Harriet up!

Knock-knock.
Who's there?
Francie.
Francie who?
Francie that!

Knock-knock.
Who's there?
Martha.
Martha who?
Martha to the beat of a different drummer!

Knock-knock.
Who's there?
Alva.
Alva who?
Alva heart!

Knock-knock.
Who's there?
Sally.
Sally who?
Sally dance?

Knock-knock.
Who's there?
Anna.
Anna who?
Anna clear day you can see forever!

Knock-knock.
Who's there?
Edna.
Edna who?
Edna the class!

Knock-knock.
Who's there?
Wendy.
Wendy who?
Wendy door opens, I'll come in!

Knock-knock.
Who's there?
Elizabeth.
Elizabeth who?
Elizabeth of knowledge is a dangerous thing!

Knock-knock.
Who's there?
Gracie.
Gracie who?
Gracie for you!

Knock-knock.
Who's there?
Bella.
Bella who?
Bella the ball.

Knock-knock.
Who's there?
Marian.
Marian who?
Marian money!

Knock-knock.
Who's there?
Maxine.
Maxine who?
Maxine the wave, dude!

Knock-knock.
Who's there?
Laverne.
Laverne who?
Laverne of catastrophe!

Knock-knock.
Who's there?
Maya.
Maya who?
Maya best friend!

Knock-knock.
Who's there?
Diane.
Diane who?
Diane to meet you!

Knock-knock.
Who's there?
Ruth.
Ruth who?
Ruth of the matter!

Knock-knock.
Who's there?
Elsie.
Elsie who?
Elsie you tomorrow!

Knock-knock.
Who's there?
Iris.
Iris who?
Iris I was rich!

Knock-knock.
Who's there?
Cassie.
Cassie who?
Cassie the forest for the trees!

Knock-knock.
Who's there?
Vanessa.
Vanessa who?
Vanessa bus is in an hour!

Knock-knock.
Who's there?
Althea.
Althea who?
Althea later, alligator!

Knock-knock.
Who's there?
Cass.
Cass who?
Cass more flies with honey than with vinegar!

Knock-knock.
Who's there?
Sonia.
Sonia who?
Sonia be another year older!

Knock-knock.
Who's there?
Rosa.
Rosa who?
Rosa corn grow in the field.

Knock-knock.
Who's there?
Phoebe.
Phoebe who?
Phoebe too expensive for me!

Knock-knock.
Who's there?
Betty.
Betty who?
Betty ya don't know who this is!

Knock-knock.
Who's there?
Greta.
Greta who?
Greta job!

Knock-knock.
Who's there?
Lily.
Lily who?
Lily house on the prairie!

Knock-knock.
Who's there?
Roxie.
Roxie who?
Roxie horror picture show!

Knock-knock.
Who's there?
Shirley.
Shirley who?
Shirley, you're joking!

Knock-knock.
Who's there?
Carrie.
Carrie who?
Carrie the groceries into the house!

Knock-knock.
Who's there?
Mae.
Mae who?
Mae be I'll tell you, and maybe I won't!

Knock-knock.
Who's there?
Edith.
Edith who?
Edith, it'll make you feel better!

Knock-knock.
Who's there?
Celeste.
Celeste who?
Celeste time I knock on this door!

Knock-knock.
Who's there?
Doris.
Doris who?
Doris shut, that's why I'm knocking!

Knock-knock.
Who's there?
Twyla.
Twyla who?
Twyla light of the Gods!

Knock-knock.
Who's there?
Joan.
Joan who?
Joan't you know who I am?

Knock-knock.
Who's there?
Ella.
Ella who?
Ellaphant!

Knock-knock.
Who's there?
Ida.
Ida who?
Ida want to live without you, baby!

Knock-knock.
Who's there?
Uva.
Uva who?
Uva vacuum!

Knock-knock.
Who's there?
Helena.
Helena who?
Helena hand basket!

Knock-knock.
Who's there?
Lena.
Lena who?
Lena against the door!

Knock-knock.
Who's there?
Anita.
Anita who?
Anita new pair of jeans!

Knock-knock.
Who's there?
Clare.
Clare who?
Clare your throat before you speak!

Knock-knock.
Who's there?
Cynthia.
Cynthia who?
Cynthia won't open the door, I'll keep knocking.

Knock-knock.
Who's there?
Norma.
Norma who?
Normally I have my key!

Knock-knock.
Who's there?
Dora.
Dora who?
Dora wood!

Knock-knock.
Who's there?
Fiona.
Fiona who?
Fiona the lookout for Mom and Dad!

Knock-knock.
Who's there?
Sophia.
Sophia who?
Sophia the cat before dinner!

Knock-knock.
Who's there?
Colleen.
Colleen who?
Colleen up this mess!

Knock-knock.
Who's there?
Marie.
Marie who?
Marie the one you love most!

Knock-knock.
Who's there?
Lucrezia.
Lucrezia who?
Lucrezia your clothes!

Knock-knock.
Who's there?
Aida.
Aida who?
Aida burger!

Knock-knock.
Who's there?
Marietta.
Marietta who?
Marietta the whole cake!

Knock-knock.
Who's there?
Frances.
Frances who?
Frances hello!

20

Knock-knock.
Who's there?
Allegra.
Allegra who?
Allegra is broken!

Knock-knock.
Who's there?
Julia.
Julia who?
Julia want some milk and cookies?

Knock-knock.
Who's there?
Lillian.
Lillian who?
Lillian the garden!

Knock-knock.
Who's there?
Bette Lou.
Bette Lou who?
Bette Lou a few pounds!

Knock-knock.
Who's there?
Nadia.
Nadia who?
Nadia head!

Knock-knock.
Who's there?
Sharon.
Sharon who?
Sharon things is generous!

Knock-knock.
Who's there?
Stella.
Stella who?
Stella want to go home!

Knock-knock.
Who's there?
Emma.
Emma who?
Emma tired!

Knock-knock.
Who's there?
Imogen.
Imogen who?
Imogen life without friends!

Knock-knock.
Who's there?
Annie.
Annie who?
Annie way you want it!

Knock-knock.
Who's there?
Frida.
Frida who?
Frida be!

Knock-knock.
Who's there?
Rosina.
Rosina who?
Rosina vase!

Knock-knock.
Who's there?
Wilma.
Wilma who?
Wilma be home for dinner?

Knock-knock.
Who's there?
Sue.
Sue who?
Sue whomever you want!

Knock-knock.
Who's there?
Zinka.
Zinka who?
Zinka the ship!

Knock-knock.
Who's there?
Robin.
Robin who?
Robin the cradle!

26

Knock-knock.
Who's there?
Irene.
Irene who?
Irene and Irene but nobody will open the door.

Knock-knock.
Who's there?
Clara.
Clara who?
Clara place at the table, I'm hungry!

Knock-knock.
Who's there?
Anna.
Anna who?
Anna one, Anna two . . .

Knock-knock.
Who's there?
Janet.
Janet who?
Janetor in a drum!

Knock-knock.
Who's there?
Paula.
Paula who?
Paula the handle and the door will open!

Knock-knock.
Who's there?
Esther.
Esther who?
Esther a doctor in the house?

Knock-knock.
Who's there?
Denise.
Denise who?
Denise are a part of your legs.

Knock-knock.
Who's there?
Alexia.
Alexia who?
Alexia again to open this door.

Knock-knock.
Who's there?
Sherry.
Sherry who?
Sherry your lunch and I'll be your friend!

Knock-knock.
Who's there?
Julia.
Julia who?
Julia think it'll rain?

Knock-knock.
Who's there?
Sandy.
Sandy who?
Sandy door, I just got a splinter!

Knock-knock.
Who's there?
Maria.
Maria who?
Maria me, I love you!

29

Knock-knock.
Who's there?
Lisa.
Lisa who?
Lisa new car for under four hundred dollars a month!

Knock-knock.
Who's there?
Cathy.
Cathy who?
Cathy the doorbell, it's too dark out here!

Knock-knock.
Who's there?
Kristin.
Kristin who?
Kristin the baby in church!

Knock-knock.
Who's there?
Marilyn.
Marilyn who?
Marilyn is a state north of Virginia.

Knock-knock.
Who's there?
Marcia.
Marcia who?
Marcia glad I stopped by?

Knock-knock.
Who's there?
Juliet.
Juliet who?
Juliet me in or not?

Knock-knock.
Who's there?
Donna.
Donna who?
Donna keep me waiting out here!

Knock-knock.
Who's there?
Rena.
Rena who?
Rena this bell doesn't do any good!

Knock-knock.
Who's there?
Barbara.
Barbara who?
Barbara of Seville!

Knock-knock.
Who's there?
Ellen.
Ellen who?
Ellenmentary, my dear Watson!

Knock-knock.
Who's there?
Phyllis.
Phyllis who?
Phyllis glass up with water, I'm thirsty!

Knock-knock.
Who's there?
Eunice.
Eunice who?
Eunice boy, let me in!

Knock-knock.
Who's there?
Mary.
Mary who?
Mary Christmas!

Knock-knock.
Who's there?
Elaine.
Elaine who?
Elaine of the freeway!

Knock-knock.
Who's there?
Audrey.
Audrey who?
Audrey to be doing this?

Knock-knock.
Who's there?
Bea.
Bea who?
Beatle Bailey!

33

Knock-knock.
Who's there?
Jilly.
Jilly who?
Jilly out here, isn't it?

Knock-knock.
Who's there?
Nan.
Nan who?
Nanswer me, or I'll go away!

Knock-knock.
Who's there?
Pat.
Pat who?
Pat yourself on the back!

Knock-knock.
Who's there?
Pammy.
Pammy who?
Pammy the key, the door is locked!

Knock-knock.
Who's there?
Etta.
Etta who?
Ettaquette!

Knock-knock.
Who's there?
Bridget.
Bridget who?
Bridget over troubled waters!

Woody Ya Open
the Door, Please?
—Boys' Names

Knock-knock.
Who's there?
Abbott.
Abbott who?
Abbott time you answered the door.

Knock-knock.
Who's there?
Arthur.
Arthur who?
Arthur any cookies in the jar?

Knock-knock.
Who's there?
Kent.
Kent who?
Kent you let me in?

Knock-knock.
Who's there?
Adam.
Adam who?
Adam if I do and Adam if I don't.

Knock-knock.
Who's there?
Alfred.
Alfred who?
Alfred of the dark!

Knock-knock.
Who's there?
Albert.
Albert who?
Albert you don't know who this is!

Knock-knock.
Who's there?
Arnie.
Arnie who?
Arnie having fun?

Knock-knock.
Who's there?
Hugh.
Hugh who?
Hugh made me love you!

Knock-knock.
Who's there?
Allan.
Allan who?
Alland of Manhattan!

Knock-knock.
Who's there?
Hugo.
Hugo who?
Hugo first, I'm scared!

Knock-knock.
Who's there?
Thomas.
Thomas who?
Thomas happy fella!

Knock-knock.
Who's there?
Clarence.
Clarence who?
Clarence sale!

Knock-knock.
Who's there?
Felix.
Felix who?
Felix the doorbell, it's broken!

Knock-knock.
Who's there?
James.
James who?
James people play!

Knock-knock.
Who's there?
Samuel.
Samuel who?
Samuel is sure stubborn!

41

Knock-knock.
Who's there?
Morrison.
Morrison who?
Morrison, more sun tan!

Knock-knock.
Who's there?
Aaron.
Aaron who?
Aaron the side of caution!

Knock-knock.
Who's there?
Alfie.
Alfie who?
Alfie you later.

Knock-knock.
Who's there?
Sam.
Sam who?
Sam day my prince will come!

Knock-knock.
Who's there?
Harold.
Harold who?
Harold do you think I am?

Knock-knock.
Who's there?
Huey.
Huey who?
Huey too much!

Knock-knock.
Who's there?
Carl.
Carl who?
Carl get you there faster than a bike!

Knock-knock.
Who's there?
Cyril.
Cyril who?
Cyril nice to meet you!

Knock-knock.
Who's there?
Adlai.
Adlai who?
Adlai in bed all day long if I could!

Knock-knock.
Who's there?
Louis.
Louis who?
Louis'n up!

Knock-knock.
Who's there?
Douglas.
Douglas who?
Douglas is broken!

Knock-knock.
Who's there?
Chester.
Chester who?
Chester the nick of time!

Knock-knock.
Who's there?
Foster.
Foster who?
Foster than the speed of light!

Knock-knock.
Who's there?
Dwight.
Dwight who?
Dwight of the living dead!

Knock-knock.
Who's there?
Gerald.
Gerald who?
Gerald shook up!

Knock-knock.
Who's there?
Colin.
Colin who?
Colin collect!

Knock-knock.
Who's there?
Lloyd.
Lloyd who?
Lloyd a horse to water, but you can't make him drink!

Knock-knock.
Who's there?
Asa.
Asa who?
Asaint among men!

Knock-knock.
Who's there?
Marcus.
Marcus who?
Marcus a book in the Bible!

Knock-knock.
Who's there?
Esau.
Esau who?
Esau down the road!

Knock-knock.
Who's there?
Jerome.
Jerome who?
Jerome where you want to!

Knock-knock.
Who's there?
Evan.
Evan who?
Evan and earth!

Knock-knock.
Who's there?
Luther.
Luther who?
Luther the silver lining!

Knock-knock.
Who's there?
Wade.
Wade who?
Wade till next time!

51

Knock-knock.
Who's there?
Tecumseh.
Tecumseh who?
Tecumseh time when all men must die!

Knock-knock.
Who's there?
Eli.
Eli who?
Eli, Eli, O!

Knock-knock.
Who's there?
Hank.
Hank who?
Hank you!

Knock-knock.
Who's there?
Shelby.
Shelby who?
Shelby comin' round the mountain when she comes!

Knock-knock.
Who's there?
Alvin.
Alvin who?
Alvin a good time, how 'bout you?

Knock-knock.
Who's there?
Ethan.
Ethan who?
Ethan me out of house and home!

Knock-knock.
Who's there?
Gabe.
Gabe who?
Gabe it my all!

Knock-knock.
Who's there?
Raoul.
Raoul who?
Raoul of law!

Knock-knock.
Who's there?
Saul.
Saul who?
Saul there is!

Knock-knock.
Who's there?
Yehuda.
Yehuda who?
Yehuda danced all night!

Knock-knock.
Who's there?
Sherwood.
Sherwood who?
Sherwood be nice to be rich!

Knock-knock.
Who's there?
Johann.
Johann who?
Johann a beautiful smile!

Knock-knock.
Who's there?
Stefan.
Stefan who?
Stefan the gas!

Knock-knock.
Who's there?
Yuri.
Yuri who?
Yuri swell friend.

Knock-knock.
Who's there?
Juan.
Juan who?
Juan to hear some more knock-knock jokes?

Knock-knock.
Who's there?
Eddie.
Eddie who?
Eddie one you want me to be!

Knock-knock.
Who's there?
Conyers.
Conyers who?
Conyers please open the door!

Knock-knock.
Who's there?
Frederick.
Frederick who?
Frederick Express!

Knock-knock.
Who's there?
Donovan.
Donovan who?
Donovan know your name!

Knock-knock.
Who's there?
Harry.
Harry who?
Harry you been?

Knock-knock.
Who's there?
Jess.
Jess who?
I give up!

Knock-knock.
Who's there?
Gus.
Gus who?
Gus you don't want to play?

Knock-knock.
Who's there?
Costa.
Costa who?
Costa lot!

Knock-knock.
Who's there?
Herman.
Herman who?
Herman is handsome!

Knock-knock.
Who's there?
Horatio.
Horatio who?
Horatio to the corner!

Knock-knock.
Who's there?
Isaac.
Isaac who?
Isaacly who do you *think* this is?

Knock-knock.
Who's there?
Albert.
Albert who?
Albert you can't eat just one!

Knock-knock.
Who's there?
Kenneth.
Kenneth who?
Kenneth be true?

Knock-knock.
Who's there?
Walter.
Walter who?
Walter wall carpeting!

Knock-knock.
Who's there?
Willi.
Willi who?
Willi be happy?

Knock-knock.
Who's there?
Hans.
Hans who?
Hans off the table!

Knock-knock.
Who's there?
Pablo.
Pablo who?
Pablo your horn.

Knock-knock.
Who's there?
Aldo.
Aldo who?
Aldo anywhere with you.

Knock-knock.
Who's there?
Raymond.
Raymond who?
Raymond me to buy milk!

Knock-knock.
Who's there?
Justin.
Justin who?
Justin time!

Knock-knock.
Who's there?
Oscar.
Oscar who?
Oscar for a date!

Knock-knock.
Who's there?
Thurston.
Thurston who?
Thurston and hungerin'!

Knock-knock.
Who's there?
Seymour.
Seymour who?
Seymour with your glasses on!

Knock-knock.
Who's there?
Giovanni.
Giovanni who?
Giovanni go to a movie?

Knock-knock.
Who's there?
Witold.
Witold who?
Witold you what to do!

Knock-knock.
Who's there?
Sebastian.
Sebastian who?
Sebastian of the community.

Knock-knock.
Who's there?
Isadore.
Isadore who?
Isadore necessary?

Knock-knock.
Who's there?
Emil.
Emil who?
Emil for the poor!

Knock-knock.
Who's there?
Zubin.
Zubin who?
Zubin eating garlic again!

Knock-knock.
Who's there?
Jussi.
Jussi who?
Jussi fruit!

Knock-knock.
Who's there?
Istvan.
Istvan who?
Istvan to be alone!

Knock-knock.
Who's there?
Andrew.
Andrew who?
Andrew a picture!

Knock-knock.
Who's there?
Giuseppe.
Giuseppe who?
Giuseppe my apology?

Knock-knock.
Who's there?
Colin.
Colin who?
Colin on the phone!

Knock-knock.
Who's there?
Mischa.
Mischa who?
Mischa a lot.

Knock-knock.
Who's there?
Maxwell.
Maxwell who?
Maxwell call later!

Knock-knock.
Who's there?
Wilfrid.
Wilfrid who?
Wilfrid like his present?

Knock-knock.
Who's there?
Alfred.
Alfred who?
Alfred the dog!

Knock-knock.
Who's there?
Frank.
Frank who.
Franks and beans!

Knock-knock.
Who's there?
Woody.
Woody who?
Woody ya open the door, please?

Knock-knock.
Who's there?
Toby.
Toby who?
Toby or not to be, that is the question!

Knock-knock.
Who's there?
Arnold.
Arnold who?
Arnold you tired of all these knock-knock jokes?

Knock-knock.
Who's there?
Al.
Al who?
Al give you some candy if you open the door!

Knock-knock.
Who's there?
Mikey.
Mikey who?
Mikey won't fit in this lock!

Knock-knock.
Who's there?
John.
John who?
John me for a soda.

Knock-knock.
Who's there?
Paul.
Paul who?
Paul a dog's tail and he'll bite you!

Knock-knock.
Who's there?
Marvin.
Marvin who?
Marvin I wonderful?

Knock-knock.
Who's there?
Alex.
Alex who?
Alex you again, knock-knock.
Who's there?
Alex.
Alex who?
Alex ask you *again*, knock-knock . .

Knock-knock.
Who's there?
Mort.
Mort who?
Mort to the point, who are you?

Knock-knock.
Who's there?
Lenny.
Lenny who?
Lenny in, I'm hungry.

Knock-knock.
Who's there?
Arthur.
Arthur who?
Arthur any kids in there who can come out to play?

Knock-knock.
Who's there?
Kendall.
Kendall who?
Kendall and Barbie go together.

Knock-knock.
Who's there?
Andrew.
Andrew who?
Andrew ride a bike?

Knock-knock.
Who's there?
Robert.
Robert who?
Roberts and burglars will steal you blind.

Knock-knock.
Who's there?
Ken.
Ken who?
Ken you see me?

Knock-knock.
Who's there?
Abe.
Abe who?
Abe-C-D-E-F-G!

Knock-knock.
Who's there?
Stevie.
Stevie who?
Stevie on?

Knock-knock.
Who's there?
Randy.
Randy who?
Randy four-minute mile!

Knock-knock.
Who's there?
Kevin.
Kevin who?
Kevin we watch some TV?

Knock-knock.
Who's there?
Cy.
Cy who?
Cy'n on the bottom line.

Knock-knock.
Who's there?
Neal.
Neal who?
Neal and pray!

Knock-knock.
Who's there?
Chuck.
Chuck who?
Chuck and see if the door is unlocked!

Knock-knock.
Who's there?
Ron.
Ron who?
Ron dinnertime, give me a call.

Knock-knock.
Who's there?
Cliff.
Cliff who?
Cliff the hedges!

Knock-knock.
Who's there?
Doug.
Doug who?
Doug good deeds and you'll go to heaven.

Aesop I Saw a Pussycat— Famous People

Knock-knock.
Who's there?
Beethoven.
Beethoven who?
Beethoven is too hot!

Knock-knock.
Who's there?
Bach.
Bach who?
Bach of cookies!

Knock-knock.
Who's there?
Chopin.
Chopin who?
Chopin the supermarket!

Knock-knock.
Who's there?
Mozart.
Mozart who?
Mozart is in the museum!

Knock-knock.
Who's there?
Vivaldi.
Vivaldi who?
Vivaldi books, there's nothing to read?

Knock-knock.
Who's there?
Handel.
Handel who?
Handel with care!

Knock-knock.
Who's there?
Schubert.
Schubert who?
Schubert I can!

Knock-knock.
Who's there?
Liszt!
Liszt who?
Liszt of ingredients!

Knock-knock.
Who's there?
Verdi.
Verdi who?
Verdi been all day?

Knock-knock.
Who's there?
Philip.
Philip who?
Philip the glass!

Knock-knock.
Who's there?
Ginastera.
Ginastera who?
Ginastera at the people!

Knock-knock.
Who's there?
Godunov.
Godunov who?
Godunov to eat!

Knock-knock.
Who's there?
Haydn.
Haydn who?
Haydn in the closet!

Knock-knock.
Who's there?
Bush.
Bush who?
Bush your money where your mouth is!

Knock-knock.
Who's there?
Farrah.
Farrah who?
Farrah 'nough!

Knock-knock.
Who's there?
Cher.
Cher who?
Cher and share alike!

Knock-knock.
Who's there?
Stalin.
Stalin who?
Stalin for time!

Knock-knock.
Who's there?
Aaron.
Aaron who?
Aaron your head!

Knock-knock.
Who's there?
Bera.
Bera who?
Bera necessity!

Knock-knock.
Who's there?
Ali.
Ali who?
Ali, Ali oxen free!

Knock-knock.
Who's there?
Tyson.
Tyson who?
Tyson of this on for size!

Knock-knock.
Who's there?
Kareem.
Kareem who?
Kareem of the crop!

Knock-knock.
Who's there?
Gipper.
Gipper who?
Gipper your best!

Knock-knock.
Who's there?
Borg.
Borg who?
Borg out of my mind!

Knock-knock.
Who's there?
Jagger.
Jagger who?
Jaggered edge!

Knock-knock.
Who's there?
Albee.
Albee who?
Albee a monkey's uncle!

Knock-knock.
Who's there?
Ferrer.
Ferrer who?
Ferrer'vrything there is a season!

81

Knock-knock.
Who's there?
Atlas.
Atlas who?
Atlas you answered the door!

Knock-knock.
Who's there?
Dali.
Dali who?
Dali've me alone!

Knock-knock.
Who's there?
Gabor.
Gabor who?
Gaborn to shop!

Knock-knock.
Who's there?
De Niro.
De Niro who!
De Niro I am to you, the more I love you!

Knock-knock.
Who's there?
Fonda.
Fonda who?
Fonda you!

Knock-knock.
Who's there?
Gable.
Gable who?
Gable to leap tall buildings in a single bound!

Knock-knock.
Who's there?
Grant.
Grant who?
Grant me a wish!

Knock-knock.
Who's there?
Hepburn.
Hepburn who?
Hepburn and indigestion!

Knock-knock.
Who's there?
Harlow.
Harlow who?
Harlow will you go?

Knock-knock.
Who's there?
Ford.
Ford who?
Ford he's a jolly good fellow!

Knock-knock.
Who's there?
Reagan.
Reagan who?
Reagan maniac.

Knock-knock.
Who's there?
Tsongas.
Tsongas who?
Tsongas you're here, let's tell some knock-knock jokes.

Knock-knock.
Who's there?
Astor.
Astor who?
Astor the ball is over!

Knock-knock.
Who's there?
Rather.
Rather who?
Rather not!

Knock-knock.
Who's there?
Cronkite.
Cronkite who?
Cronkite evidence!

Knock-knock.
Who's there?
Aesop.
Aesop who?
Aesop I saw a pussycat!

Knock-knock.
Who's there?
Tolkien.
Tolkien who?
Tolkiens get you on the subway.

Knock-knock.
Who's there?
Oates.
Oates who?
Oates'ay can you see!

Knock-knock.
Who's there?
Spillane.
Spillane who?
Spillane that knock-knock joke!

Knock-knock.
Who's there?
Cash.
Cash who.
Cash me if you can!

Knock-knock.
Who's there?
Wynette.
Wynette who?
Wynette let me in?

Knock-knock.
Who's there?
Anka.
Anka who?
Anka the ship!

Knock-knock.
Who's there?
Aretha.
Aretha who?
Aretha flowers!

Knock-knock.
Who's there?
Bolton.
Bolton who?
Bolton the door!

Knock-knock.
Who's there?
Sondheim.
Sondheim who?
Sondheim soon!

Knock-knock.
Who's there?
Cugat.
Cugat who?
Cugat to love my knock-knock jokes!

Knock-knock.
Who's there?
Iglesias.
Iglesias who?
Iglesias idea I ever heard!

Knock-knock.
Who's there?
Sinatra.
Sinatra who?
Sinatra be a law!

Knock-knock.
Who's there?
Saddam.
Saddam who?
Saddam and shut up!

Knock-knock.
Who's there?
Coolidge.
Coolidge who?
Coolidge a cucumber!

Knock-knock.
Who's there?
Koch.
Koch who?
Koch in the act!

Knock-knock.
Who's there?
Dinah.
Dinah who?
Dinah'mals are at the zoo.

Knock-knock.
Who's there?
Parton.
Parton who?
Parton my French!

Knock-knock.
Who's there?
Austen.
Austen who?
Austen corrected!

Knock-knock.
Who's there?
Burns.
Burns who?
Burns me up!

Knock-knock.
Who's there?
Spock.
Spock who?
Spock louder!

Knock-knock.
Who's there?
Cicero.
Cicero who?
Cicero the boat ashore!

Knock-knock.
Who's there?
Axl.
Axl who?
Axl me nicely and I'll tell you!

Knock-knock.
Who's there?
Lincoln.
Lincoln who?
Lincoln logs!

Knock-knock.
Who's there?
Desi.
Desi who?
Desi-gnated hitter!

Knock-knock.
Who's there?
Yoda.
Yoda who?
Yoda le-lee-who!

Knock-knock.
Who's there?
Donatello.
Donatello who?
Donatellon me!

Knock-knock.
Who's there?
Ivana.
Ivana who?
Ivana be rich!

Knock-knock.
Who's there?
Leona.
Leona who?
Leonaly way to go!

Knock-knock.
Who's there?
Whoopi.
Whoopi who?
Whoopi cushion!

Bacon a Cake
for Your Birthday
—Food

Knock-knock.
Who's there?
Celery.
Celery who?
Celery me your lunch for a quarter!

Knock-knock.
Who's there?
Orange.
Orange who?
Orange you even going to open the door?

Knock-knock.
Who's there?
Lemon.
Lemon who?
Lemon me give you a kiss!

Knock-knock.
Who's there?
Lime.
Lime who?
Lime bean!

Knock-knock.
Who's there?
Chicken.
Chicken who?
Chicken the oven, I think something's burning.

Knock-knock.
Who's there?
Soup.
Soup who?
Superman!

Knock-knock.
Who's there?
Apple.
Apple who?
Apple your hair if you don't let me in!

Knock-knock.
Who's there?
Bacon.
Bacon who?
Bacon a cake for your birthday!

Knock-knock.
Who's there?
Butter.
Butter who?
Butter bring an umbrella, it looks like rain.

Knock-knock.
Who's there?
Carrot.
Carrot who?
Carrot me back to Old Virginia!

Knock-knock.
Who's there?
Chow mein.
Chow mein who?
Chow mein to meet you, my dear!

Knock-knock.
Who's there?
Egg.
Egg who?
Egg-citing to meet you, my dear!

Knock-knock.
Who's there?
Falafel.
Falafel who?
Falafel my bike and broke my arm!

Knock-knock.
Who's there?
Ketchup.
Ketchup who?
Ketchup the tree again!

Knock-knock.
Who's there?
Olive.
Olive who?
Olive you!

Knock-knock.
Who's there?
Omelet.
Omelet who?
Omelet'in you kiss me.

Knock-knock.
Who's there?
Pizza.
Pizza who?
Pizza the pie!

Knock-knock.
Who's there?
Toast.
Toast who?
Toast were the days!

Knock-knock.
Who's there?
Tuna.
Tuna who?
Tuna in tomorrow!

Knock-knock.
Who's there?
Wine.
Wine who?
Wine don't you like knock-knock jokes?

Knock-knock.
Who's there?
Avocado.
Avocado who?
Avocado a cold!

Knock-knock.
Who's there?
Bean.
Bean who?
Bean fishin' lately?

Knock-knock.
Who's there?
Beets.
Beets who?
Beets me!

Knock-knock.
Who's there?
Brie.
Brie who?
Brie me the head of John the Baptist!

Knock-knock.
Who's there?
Plums.
Plums who?
Plums me you'll always love me!

Knock-knock.
Who's there?
Cherry.
Cherry who?
Cherry Lewis!

Knock-knock.
Who's there?
Curry.
Curry who?
Curry me back to Old Virginia!

Knock-knock.
Who's there?
Dill.
Dill who?
Dill we meet again!

Knock-knock.
Who's there?
Figs.
Figs who?
Figs the doorbell, it's broken.

Knock-knock.
Who's there?
Fruit.
Fruit who?
Fruit of the Loom!

Knock-knock.
Who's there?
Goose.
Goose who?
Goose see a doctor, you look sick.

Knock-knock.
Who's there?
Grapes.
Grapes who?
Grapes Suzette!

Knock-knock.
Who's there?
Gravy.
Gravy who?
Gravy Crockett!

Knock-knock.
Who's there?
Halibut.
Halibut who?
Halibut a kiss, sweetie!

Knock-knock.
Who's there?
Ice cream.
Ice cream who?
Ice cream of Jeannie!

Knock-knock.
Who's there?
Muffin.
Muffin who?
Muffin wrong with me, how 'bout you?

Knock-knock.
Who's there?
Okra.
Okra who?
Okra Winfrey!

Knock-knock.
Who's there?
Peas.
Peas who?
Peas of the rock!

Knock-knock.
Who's there?
Pears.
Pears who?
Pears the party?

105

Knock-knock.
Who's there?
Pecan.
Pecan who?
Pecan someone your own size!

Knock-knock.
Who's there?
Salmon.
Salmon who?
Salmonchanted evening.

Knock-knock.
Who's there?
Sherbet.
Sherbet who?
Sherbet Forest!

Knock-knock.
Who's there?
Turnip.
Turnip who?
Turnip the volume, I can't hear.

Quebec to Where
You Came From
—Places

Knock-knock.
Who's there?
Lodz.
Lodz who?
Lodz of fun!

Knock-knock.
Who's there?
Ottawa.
Ottawa who?
Ottawa to go to bed!

Knock-knock.
Who's there?
Glasgow.
Glasgow who?
Glasgow to the movies!

Knock-knock.
Who's there?
Beirut.
Beirut who?
Beirut force!

Knock-knock.
Who's there?
Mecca.
Mecca who?
Mecca me happy!

Knock-knock.
Who's there?
Essen.
Essen who?
Essen it fun to hear knock-knock jokes?

Knock-knock.
Who's there?
Tunis.
Tunis who?
Tunis company, three's a crowd!

Knock-knock.
Who's there?
Tripoli.
Tripoli who?
Tripoli play!

Knock-knock.
Who's there?
Fez.
Fez who?
Fez me, that who!

Knock-knock.
Who's there?
Kyoto.
Kyoto who?
Kyoto jail, do not pass Go!

Knock-knock.
Who's there?
Minsk.
Minsk who?
Minsk meat!

Knock-knock.
Who's there?
Medellin.
Medellin who?
Medellin where you don't belong!

Knock-knock.
Who's there?
Gorky.
Gorky who?
Gorky will unlock the door!

Knock-knock.
Who's there?
Odessa.
Odessa who?
Odessa good knock-knock joke!

Knock-knock.
Who's there?
Munich.
Munich who?
Munich me sick!

Knock-knock.
Who's there?
Giza.
Giza who?
Giza nice boy!

Knock-knock.
Who's there?
Sofia.
Sofia who?
Sofia me, I'm hungry!

Knock-knock.
Who's there?
Turin.
Turin who?
Turin to a vampire on Halloween!

Knock-knock.
Who's there?
Perth.
Perth who?
Perth your lips and whistle!

Knock-knock.
Who's there?
Leon.
Leon who?
Leonly one for me!

Knock-knock.
Who's there?
Lisbon.
Lisbon who?
Lisbon married eight times!

Knock-knock.
Who's there?
Halifax.
Halifax who?
Halifax you, if you'll fax me!

Knock-knock.
Who's there?
Ghent.
Ghent who?
Ghent out of here!

Knock-knock.
Who's there?
Haifa.
Haifa who?
Haifa dollar is better than none!

Knock-knock.
Who's there?
Seoul.
Seoul who?
Seoul food!

Knock-knock.
Who's there?
Teheran.
Teheran who?
Teheran up the road!

Knock-knock.
Who's there?
Delhi.
Delhi who?
Delhicatessen!

Knock-knock.
Who's there?
Ankara.
Ankara who?
Ankara went off the cliff!

Knock-knock.
Who's there?
Athens.
Athens who?
Athens I love you!

Knock-knock.
Who's there?
Toronto.
Toronto who?
Toronto be a law against knock-knock jokes!

Knock-knock.
Who's there?
Rome.
Rome who?
Rome is where the heart is!

Knock-knock.
Who's there?
Taipei.
Taipei who?
Taipei sixty words a minute is pretty fast!

Knock-knock.
Who's there?
Paris.
Paris who?
Paris the thought!

Knock-knock.
Who's there?
Havana.
Havana who?
Havana good time?

Knock-knock.
Who's there?
India.
India who?
Indiafternoon I get sleepy!

Knock-knock.
Who's there?
Oman.
Oman who?
Oman, are you cute!

Knock-knock.
Who's there?
Laos.
Laos who?
Laos and found!

Knock-knock.
Who's there?
Mali.
Mali who?
Mali Brown!

Knock-knock.
Who's there?
Congo.
Congo who?
Congo out, I'm grounded!

Knock-knock.
Who's there?
Benin.
Benin who?
Benin shopping lately?

Knock-knock.
Who's there?
Ghana.
Ghana who?
Ghana dance!

Knock-knock.
Who's there?
Uganda.
Uganda who?
Uganda see a movie?

Knock-knock.
Who's there?
Zaire.
Zaire who?
Zaire is polluted!

Knock-knock.
Who's there?
Kenya.
Kenya who?
Kenya guess who it is?

Knock-knock.
Who's there?
Guinea.
Guinea who?
Guinea a break!

Knock-knock.
Who's there?
Chad.
Chad who?
Chad to make your acquaintance!

Knock-knock.
Who's there?
Haiti.
Haiti who?
Haiti see a good thing go to waste!

Knock-knock.
Who's there?
Belize.
Belize who?
Belize in yourself!

Knock-knock.
Who's there?
Bolzano.
Bolzano who?
Bolzano the door!

Knock-knock.
Who's there?
Japan.
Japan who?
Japan is too hot!

Knock-knock.
Who's there?
Bologna.
Bologna who?
Bologna and cheese!

Knock-knock.
Who's there?
Italy.
Italy who?
Italy be a big job!

Knock-knock.
Who's there?
Lucerne.
Lucerne who?
Lucerne multiplication today?

Knock-knock.
Who's there?
Sweden.
Sweden who?
Sweden the coffee!

Knock-knock.
Who's there?
Egypt.
Egypt who?
Egypt me out of money!

Knock-knock.
Who's there?
Chile.
Chile who?
Chile out tonight!

Knock-knock.
Who's there?
Alba.
Alba who?
Alba in the next room for a while!

Knock-knock.
Who's there?
Austin.
Austin who?
Austin I forget things!

Knock-knock.
Who's there?
Peru.
Peru who?
Peru your point!

Knock-knock.
Who's there?
Berlin.
Berlin who?
Berlin the water for pasta!

Knock-knock.
Who's there?
Seville.
Seville who?
Seville you play with me?

Knock-knock.
Who's there?
Galway.
Galway who?
Galway, you bother me!

Knock-knock.
Who's there?
Alaska.
Alaska who?
Alaska again, please let me in.

Knock-knock.
Who's there?
Hawaii.
Hawaii who?
Hawaii doin'?

Knock-knock.
Who's there?
Texas.
Texas who?
Texas are getting higher every year!

Knock-knock.
Who's there?
Florida.
Florida who?
Florida bathroom is wet.

Knock-knock.
Who's there?
Idaho.
Idaho who?
Idaho'd the whole garden, but I was tired.

Knock-knock.
Who's there?
Montana.
Montana who?
Montana your hide if she finds out you broke the clock.

Knock-knock.
Who's there?
Wyoming.
Wyoming who?
Wyoming so mean to me?

Knock-knock.
Who's there?
Utah.
Utah who?
Utahld me to knock before I entered a room.

Knock-knock.
Who's there?
Nebraska.
Nebraska who?
Nebraska girl for a date, she might say yes!

Knock-knock.
Who's there?
Iowa.
Iowa who?
Iowa you a dollar!

Knock-knock.
Who's there?
Missouri.
Missouri who?
Missouri loves company!

Knock-knock.
Who's there?
Kansas.
Kansas who?
Kansas the best way to buy tuna!

Knock-knock.
Who's there?
Arkansas.
Arkansas who?
Arkansas through any piece of wood!

Knock-knock.
Who's there?
Tennessee.
Tennessee who?
Tennessee is played at Wimbledon!

Knock-knock.
Who's there?
Ohio.
Ohio who?
Ohio to you too!

Knock-knock.
Who's there?
Indiana.
Indiana who?
Indiannals of history, you'll be famous.

Knock-knock.
Who's there?
Maine.
Maine who?
Maine I come in now?

Knock-knock.
Who's there?
Alberta.
Alberta who?
Alberta'll be over in a few minutes.

Knock-knock.
Who's there?
Manitoba.
Manitoba who?
Manitoba me hours to get here!

Knock-knock.
Who's there?
Yukon.
Yukon who?
Yukon let me in now!

Knock-knock.
Who's there?
Quebec.
Quebec who?
Quebec to where you came from!

Knock-knock.
Who's there?
Germany.
Germany who?
Germany people knock on your door?

Knock-knock.
Who's there?
France.
France who?
France of the family.

Knock-knock.
Who's there?
Russia.
Russia who?
Russia through your dinner and you'll get sick!

Knock-knock.
Who's there?
China.
China who?
China like old times, isn't it?

Knock-knock.
Who's there?
India.
India who?
Indiapartment next door is a big dog!

Knock-knock.
Who's there?
Europe.
Europe who?
Europening the door too slowly!

Knock-knock.
Who's there?
Asia.
Asia who?
Asia mother at home?

Knock-knock.
Who's there?
Sweden.
Sweden who?
Sweden sour!

Knock-knock.
Who's there?
Norway.
Norway who?
Norway will I leave until you open this door!

Knock-knock.
Who's there?
Holland.
Holland who?
Holland you going to make me wait out here?

Knock-knock.
Who's there?
Prussia.
Prussia who?
Prussia cooker!

Knock-knock.
Who's there?
Iran.
Iran who?
Iran over to see you!

Knock-knock.
Who's there?
Turkey.
Turkey who?
Turkey, open door!

Knock-knock.
Who's there?
Spain.
Spain who?
Spain to have to keep knocking on this door!

About the Author

Dora Wood lives in New York.